970L

NEVADA

The Silver State

BY
JOHN HAMILTON

Abdo & Daughters

An imprint of Abdo Publishing | abdopublishing.com

abdopublishing.com

Published by ABDO Publishing, a division of ABDO, PO Box 398166, Minneapolis, Minnesota 55439. Copyright © 2017 by Abdo Consulting Group, Inc. International copyrights reserved in all countries. No part of this book may be reproduced in any form without written permission from the publisher. ABDO & Daughters™ is a trademark and logo of ABDO Publishing.

Printed in the United States of America, North Mankato, Minnesota.
042016
092016

Editor: Sue Hamilton   **Contributing Editor:** Bridget O'Brien
Graphic Design: Sue Hamilton
Cover Art Direction: Candice Keimig   **Cover Photo Selection:** Neil Klinepier
Cover Photo: iStock
Interior Images: Alamy, AP, Corbis, Dreamstime, Edward Curtis, Excalibur Hotel And Casino/Erik Kabik, Granger Collection, Heinrich Harder, iStock, John Hamilton, Las Vegas 51s, Library of Congress, Mile High Maps, Minden Pictures, The Mob Museum, Mountain High Maps, National Park Service, Nevada Legislature, New York Public Library, Reno Aces, Reno Bighorns Science Source, Tim O'Brien, U.S. Air Force, Virginia City Tourism Commission, & Wikimedia.

Statistics: *State and City Populations*, U.S. Census Bureau, July 1, 2015/2014 estimates; *Land and Water Area*, U.S. Census Bureau, 2010 Census, MAF/TIGER database; *State Temperature Extremes*, NOAA National Climatic Data Center; *Climatology and Average Annual Precipitation*, NOAA National Climatic Data Center, 1980-2015 statewide averages; *State Highest and Lowest Points*, NOAA National Geodetic Survey.

Websites: To learn more about the United States, visit booklinks.abdopublishing.com. These links are routinely monitored and updated to provide the most current information available.

Cataloging-in-Publication Data

Names: Hamilton, John, 1959- author.
Title: Nevada / by John Hamilton.
Description: Minneapolis, MN : Abdo Publishing, [2017] | Series: The United
    States of America | Includes index.
Identifiers: LCCN 2015957620 | ISBN 9781680783308 (lib. bdg.) |
    ISBN 9781680774344 (ebook)
Subjects: LCSH: Nevada--Juvenile literature.
Classification: DDC 979.3--dc23
LC record available at http://lccn.loc.gov/2015957620

CONTENTS

THE SILVER STATE

Nevada is a land of contrasts. The cities of Las Vegas and Reno shine with neon-lit entertainment and high-energy opportunity. But most of Nevada is rural, with people spread out in small towns. Along the state's western border with California is the Sierra Nevada mountain range, the state's namesake, with forested, snow-capped peaks reaching to the sky. Natural beauty is all around. Yet Nevada contains deserts so rugged and torturously hot they remain uninhabited.

Nevada has a rich history that started in the Old West. Vast fortunes were made in the 1800s as miners dug huge amounts of silver and gold from the Earth. Nevada's nickname, "The Silver State," is a reminder of the state's mining heritage. Nevada is a top producer of silver, and the number-one producer of gold, in the United States today.

Las Vegas is a popular tourist destination for more than 42 million people each year.

Red Rock Canyon is a beautiful area just outside of Las Vegas, Nevada.

QUICK FACTS

Name: Nevada comes from the Spanish word *nevada*, which means "snow covered." It refers to the snow-capped peaks of the Sierra Nevada mountain range.

State Capital: Carson City, population 54,522

Date of Statehood: October 31, 1864 (36th state)

Population: 2,890,845 (35th-most populous state)

Area (Total Land and Water): 110,572 square miles (286,380 sq km), 7th-largest state

Largest City: Las Vegas, population 613,599

Nickname: Silver State; Sagebrush State; Battle-Born State

Motto: All For Our Country

State Bird: Mountain Bluebird

State Flower: Sagebrush

State Precious Gemstone: Virgin Valley Black Fire Opal

State Tree: Singleleaf Piñon and Bristlecone Pine

State Song: "Home Means Nevada"

Highest Point: Boundary Peak, 13,140 feet (4,005 m)

Lowest Point: Colorado River, 479 feet (146 m)

Average July High Temperature: 89°F (32°C) in the northwest, 100°F (38°C) in the south

Record High Temperature: 125°F (52°C), in Laughlin on June 29, 1994

Average January Low Temperature: 21°F (-6°C) in the northwest, 36°F (2°C) in the south

Record Low Temperature: -50°F (-46°C), in San Jacinto on January 8, 1937

Average Annual Precipitation: 10 inches (25 cm) in the northwest, 7 inches (18 cm) in the south

Number of U.S. Senators: 2

Number of U.S. Representatives: 4

U.S. Postal Service Abbreviation: NV

GEOGRAPHY

Most of Nevada is covered by desert, which receives little rainfall. Nevada is one of the driest states in the nation. Almost the entire state is part of a geological region called the Basin and Range Province. It also includes parts of many other Southwestern states.

The Basin and Range Province is a series of flat, dry desert valleys that alternate with steep mountain ranges. There are dozens of mountain ranges in Nevada. Most of them lie in a north-south direction. The Earth's crust has been pulled apart over millions of years, creating the basins and mountains. From space, the steep mountains look like a bunch of caterpillars marching south across a flat plain.

Most of Nevada is covered by desert that alternates with steep mountain ranges.

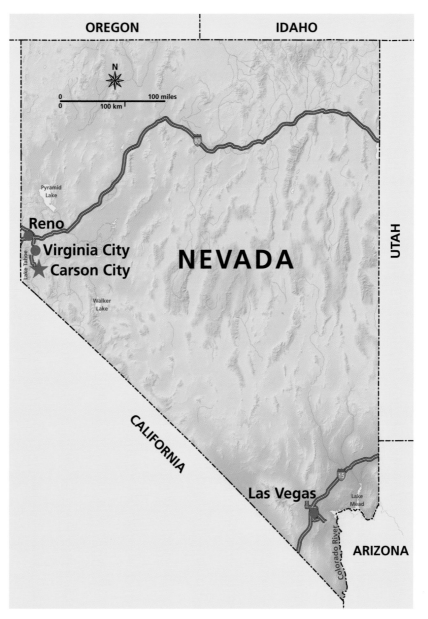

Nevada's total land and water area is 110,572 square miles (286,380 sq km). It is the 7th-largest state. The state capital is Carson City.

Within the Basin and Range Province is a region called the Great Basin. It covers most of Nevada. This water drainage system is like a giant, shallow bowl. Water in the Great Basin comes mainly from snow in the mountains that melts in the spring. The water does not make its way to the ocean. Instead, it is trapped in the basin. In the hot summer months, most of the water evaporates, leaving behind dry lakes called salt flats.

A small part of the Sierra Nevada mountain range is in Nevada. These tall, granite peaks are in a narrow strip of the west-central part of the state that borders California. Just to the south are the White Mountains, which are home to Boundary Peak, Nevada's highest point. It soars 13,140 feet (4,005 m) high.

Water in Nevada's Great Basin comes mainly from snow in the mountains that melts in the spring.

Nestled within the Sierra Nevada is Lake Tahoe, North America's largest alpine lake. At 1,645 feet (501 m) deep, it is also the second-deepest lake in the country (behind Oregon's Crater Lake). Located just west of Carson City, the Nevada-California border runs through the middle of the lake. Famous for crystal-clear blue waters, Lake Tahoe is a popular resort destination.

The southern part of Nevada is within the Mojave Desert. Las Vegas is in this region. Summers can be scorching hot. The Colorado River flows along Nevada's southeastern border with Arizona. Lake Mead is a large reservoir created by Hoover Dam on the Colorado River.

CLIMATE AND WEATHER

Nevada is a desert state because of the blocking action of the Sierra Nevada mountain range. Moisture-filled clouds blow in from the Pacific Ocean and over California. As air reaches the Nevada border, it rises to pass over the tall mountains. The moisture condenses and falls as rain or snow. The far-western mountains of Nevada can receive as much as 24 inches (61 cm) of precipitation per year. However, by the time the air passes over the rest of the state, most of the moisture has already been wrung out. Some parts of Nevada receive as little as 4 inches (10 cm) of rain annually because of this "rain shadow" effect.

In the northern and eastern parts of Nevada, winters are usually long and cold. The average January low temperature in the northwest corner of the state is 21°F (-6°C). In the south, in the Mojave Desert, summers are long and hot, with short winters. The record high temperature in Nevada occurred on June 29, 1994, in the town of Laughlin, in the far-southern part of the state. That day, the thermometer soared to 125°F (52°C).

Laughlin

CLIMATE AND WEATHER

PLANTS AND
ANIMALS

Even though Nevada may seem too hot and dry for life, there are many species of plants and animals that make the state their home. They have adapted to live in harsh environments, and can withstand extreme heat and scarce amounts of water.

In Nevada's desert areas, common plants include yucca, mesquite, creosote, and greasewood. There are more than 30 species of cactuses growing on the desert floor, including red barrel cactus, silver cholla cactus, and beavertail cactus. Sagebrush and Joshua trees are also very common.

Cactus

Joshua Tree

Bristlecone Pine

Many kinds of trees grow in Nevada's mountain forests. They include Douglas fir, ponderosa pine, and juniper trees. The singleleaf piñon pine is one of Nevada's two official state trees. They have short, stiff needles and a fragrant pine smell. The other state tree is the rare bristlecone pine. Found in high altitudes, they have thick trunks and contorted limbs. They are slow growers, well adapted to harsh conditions. They are also the oldest living things on Earth. Some Nevada bristlecone pines are at least 5,000 years old.

PLANTS AND ANIMALS

Nevada has hundreds of wildflower species. During the spring, the state's deserts and mountains often come alive with color. Nevada wildflowers include violets, shooting stars, desert marigolds, and Indian paintbrushes. The official state flower is sagebrush.

Nevada's animal species are uniquely able to live in the state's deserts and mountains. Some animals are found in both habitats. Mountain lions, also called cougars, prefer the protection of the mountain forests, but they can also roam the desert plains.

Other large mountain critters include bighorn sheep, mule deer, and elk. Pronghorn antelope prefer the open plains. Black bears and beavers live in some state forests. Smaller mammals include rabbits, coyotes, foxes, squirrels, weasels, skunks, pocket gophers, kangaroo rats, and bobcats.

Bighorn Sheep

Desert Tortoise

Western Diamondback

Gambel's Quail

Roadrunner

Nevada's desert reptiles thrive even in areas with little moisture and extreme temperatures. They include geckos, horned lizards (also called horned toads), and desert tortoises.

There are many kinds of snakes in Nevada. Most are harmless, but a few species are venomous and should be avoided. They include sidewinders, Mohave rattlesnakes, western rattlesnakes, and western diamondbacks.

Birds found soaring through Nevada's skies include quail, sage grouse, pheasants, bald eagles, hawks, and owls. Roadrunners can often be seen scampering across the desert at speeds up to 20 miles per hour (32 kph). The official state bird is the mountain bluebird.

In Nevada's 200 lakes and 600 streams and rivers can be found bass, trout, sunfish, crappie, and catfish. The official state fish is the Lahontan cutthroat trout.

PLANTS AND ANIMALS

HISTORY

P eople have lived in the Nevada area for at least 12,000 years. These Paleo-Indians were the ancestors of today's Native Americans. They developed excellent hunting and gathering skills in order to live in Nevada's harsh, dry environment.

By the 1700s, there were several Native American tribes living in Nevada. Two tribes dominated. The Shoshone lived in northeastern and central Nevada, while the Paiute occupied most of the western and southeastern areas. Other tribes included the Washoe and Walapai.

A Paiute Native American fishes from the shore at Walker Lake in western Nevada.

From 1842-1843, John C. Frémont explored the area that included Nevada's Pyramid Lake.

Francisco Garcés was probably the first European to set foot in today's Nevada. He was a Spanish missionary who explored the American Southwest in 1776. By the 1820s, other missionaries and trappers began exploring the area.

The Old Spanish Trail was a 700-mile (1,127-km) route between Santa Fe, New Mexico, and Los Angeles, California. Starting around 1830, it brought people through the southern tip of Nevada.

In 1843, explorer John Frémont mapped much of Nevada. He named the Carson River in honor of Kit Carson, his friend and fellow explorer.

John Frémont

After winning the Mexican-American War (1846-1848), the United States gained a large portion of the American Southwest, including present-day Nevada. The first European-American settlement in Nevada was Genoa, founded in 1851. A trading post built by Mormon pioneers, it was located along the Emigrant Trail, just east of Lake Tahoe.

In 1859, large amounts of silver were discovered on the east side of Mount Davidson, near Carson City. The rich find was dubbed the Comstock Lode. It was the first major silver deposit found in the United States. Gold was soon discovered in the area as well. Treasure hunters flocked to Mount Davidson and set up camps. The nearby boomtown of Virginia City sprang up seemingly overnight. Vast riches were pulled from the many mines dug into the Earth.

A cutaway view of the Comstock Lode mines in Nevada.

Rhyolite Store

Bank

Train Depot

From 1905-1910, the town of Rhyolite, Nevada, was a booming gold town. By 1919, the gold had run out and the town was abandoned. Today, it is a ghost town.

In 1864, President Abraham Lincoln urged lawmakers to recognize Nevada as a state. At the time, the country was embroiled in the Civil War (1861-1865). Lincoln knew that Nevada's mineral wealth would greatly help the Union. On October 31, 1864, Nevada became the 36th state.

In the years following statehood, Nevada was dependent on mining and cattle ranching. There were good years and bad. The price of silver declined in the 1870s. Then, when the rich veins began to run out, many mines were abandoned. Thriving communities became dusty ghost towns. In the 1880s, several harsh winters killed thousands of cattle, forcing many ranches into bankruptcy. The population of Nevada greatly declined.

In the early 1900s, Nevada's luck changed again. Big silver deposits were found in Tonopah. A gold strike occurred near the town of Goldfield, and copper was unearthed in Ely. More fortunes were made as new treasure seekers flooded into the state.

As more and more railroads were built across Nevada, it became cheaper to ship minerals and other bulky goods. The railroads also helped ranchers and farmers.

When the Great Depression left the nation's economy in shambles during the 1930s, Nevada was hit

The building of railroads in the 1800s and 1900s helped link Nevada with the rest of the country. It became cheaper to ship products such as minerals, farm produce, and livestock to locations across the United States.

hard. State lawmakers hoped to attract tourist dollars by legalizing casinos and building resorts. Their gamble paid off. With the completion of the Hoover Dam in 1936 and the construction of elaborate casinos and entertainment complexes during World War II (1939-1945), cities like Las Vegas and Reno saw their populations begin to soar.

A nuclear bomb explodes in the Nevada desert in 1952.

Starting in the 1950s, the United States military took advantage of Nevada's remote desert lands to test new aircraft and nuclear bombs. Military spending helped spur the Nevada economy, but there were dangers. About 100 above-ground nuclear bomb tests took place at Yucca Flat, a desert basin about 100 miles (161 km) northwest of Las Vegas. Scientists did not yet fully understand the hazards of radiation, and many people were unknowingly exposed. Nuclear testing eventually moved underground, and stopped altogether in 1992.

Today, Nevada's population continues to grow rapidly. Tourism is the top industry. Challenges facing the state include water conservation and making sure services, such as schools and roads, keep pace with the expanding population.

DID YOU KNOW?

• Hard-biting, venomous Gila (pronounced Hee-la) monsters are found in the southern tip of Nevada, in the Mojave Desert. They are large lizards with short legs and curved claws for digging. The slow-moving Gila monsters are seldom a danger to humans, and are protected by state law. They spend 99 percent of their lives underground. They have beaded, brightly-colored orange skin with black banding. They are the only lizards known to have grooved teeth and venom glands, which they use to hunt small mammals or birds.

• Hoover Dam was completed in 1936. It was built in Black Canyon, spanning the Colorado River between Nevada and Arizona. It stands 726 feet (221 m) tall and weighs more than 6.6 million tons (6 million metric tons). It provides enough electricity for 1.3 million people. Lake Mead is the dam's reservoir. It provides water to large parts of Nevada, Arizona, and California. The city of Las Vegas gets more than 90 percent of its water from Lake Mead. In recent years, a long drought has caused lake levels to drop, reinforcing the need to conserve water.

• In 1861, 25-year-old Samuel Clemens arrived in Virginia City. He tried his hand at silver mining, but had little luck. Instead, he became the editor of Virginia City's newspaper, *Territorial Enterprise*. It was while writing for the newspaper that he first used his famous pen name: Mark Twain.

DID YOU KNOW?

PEOPLE

Andre Agassi (1970-) was one of the most dominating tennis players in the world during the 1990s and 2000s. Many sports writers have called him one of the greatest tennis stars of all time. Agassi was born and spent his early childhood in Las Vegas, Nevada. He could serve a tennis ball on a full court by age two. He won his first professional tennis tournament in 1987. He charmed audiences with his skillful play and flashy good looks. He won a gold medal at the 1996 Summer Olympic Games in Atlanta, Georgia. He won all four Grand Slam singles events, including a win at Wimbledon, England, in 1992. Agassi retired from professional tennis in 2006.

Sarah Winnemucca (c. 1844-1891) was an author and teacher who spoke out against the mistreatment of Native Americans. She was the daughter of Winnemucca, a war chief of the Northern Paiute tribe. She was born near Humboldt Lake, in western Nevada. By the time she was 14 years old, she could speak five languages. She was an interpreter for the United States Army during the 1860s and 1870s. She toured the country giving lectures and educating people about Native Americans. She published her autobiography, *Life Among the Paiutes: Their Wrongs and Claims*, in 1883. She joined the Nevada Writers Hall of Fame in 1993.

Amy Purdy (1979-) is a top-ranked snowboarder, model, actress, and motivational speaker. She was born and grew up in Las Vegas, Nevada. As a young woman, she loved snowboarding. But when she was 19, she contracted bacterial meningitis. She survived, but both her legs were amputated. She was determined to continue snowboarding. She helped design new prosthetic legs that work well with the sport. Today, she has won several World Cup gold medals in snowboard cross, and she took home the bronze medal at the 2014 Winter Paralympics in Sochi, Russia. She also co-founded Adaptive Action Sports, a non-profit company that helps physically disabled people get involved in sports.

Pat Nixon

(1912-1993) was the wife of Richard Nixon, the 37th president of the United States. After graduating with honors from the University of Southern California in Los Angeles, California, she met her future husband at a community theater group. They married in 1940. Pat helped her husband's political career when he became a congressman in 1947, a senator in 1950, vice president in 1953, and president in 1969. As first lady, she urged people to volunteer in their communities. "Our success as a nation," she said, "depends on our willingness to give generously of ourselves for the welfare and enrichment of the lives of others." Pat Nixon was born in the mining town of Ely, Nevada.

CITIES

Las Vegas is the most populous city in Nevada. Its population is 613,599. Combined with its surrounding suburbs, the metropolitan area is home to more than 2 million people. That is more than two-thirds the population of the entire state. Early in its history, Las Vegas was a resting spot for pioneers traveling west. It officially became a city in 1911. Las Vegas grew rapidly after the 1935 completion of nearby Hoover Dam, which provided cheap hydroelectric power. Today, many businesses are located in the city. It is a major tourist spot, with casinos, live entertainment, and sporting events. There are also many museums and restaurants. The University of Nevada, Las Vegas, enrolls more than 28,000 students.

Carson City is the capital of Nevada. It is located in the west-central part of the state. Its population is 54,522. It is named after famous mountain man Kit Carson. The city was founded in 1858. It grew rapidly with the discovery of silver and gold in the area. Today, top employers include health care, local and state government, hotels, and casinos. The city is home to Western Nevada College. There are several ski resorts located in the nearby Sierra Nevada mountain range. Beautiful Lake Tahoe is west of the city.

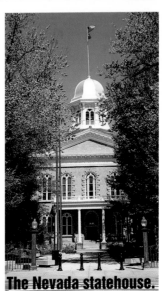

The Nevada statehouse.

Reno Air Races

Reno is located in the northwestern part of Nevada, near the California border. Its population is 236,995. In the 1840s, it was an important rest stop for pioneers on the California Trail. The population grew after silver and gold were discovered nearby. Today, Reno has many types of businesses. Top employers include education, health care, and casino resorts. Nearby ski resorts and Lake Tahoe are major attractions. The University of Nevada, Reno, is the state's oldest university, established in 1874. The annual Reno National Championship Air Races features high-performance airplanes racing against each other on a huge course at Reno-Stead Airport.

Virginia City is less than 40 miles (64 km) southeast of Reno, in western Nevada. In 1859, an enormous deposit of gold and silver was discovered in the area. Called the Comstock Lode, it eventually produced hundreds of millions of dollars in precious metals. Virginia City was founded after thousands of miners and other settlers rushed to Nevada to seek their fortunes. The mines made many people rich. The boom years led Nevada to statehood in 1864. Today, Virginia City has a population of about 850, but millions of people visit each year to shop, dine, and experience Nevada history.

TRANSPORTATION

There are 40,139 miles (64,597 km) of public roadways in Nevada, including approximately 600 miles (966 km) of Interstate highways. Interstate I-80 goes roughly east and west across northern Nevada, passing through the cities of Elko, Winnemucca, and Reno. It follows the approximate path of the California Trail and the nation's first transcontinental railroad. Interstate I-15 cuts across the very southeastern tip of Nevada, passing through the city of Las Vegas.

Nevada has thousands of miles of public roadways.

Railroads have always been an important way to transport bulky cargo, such as minerals, across Nevada. Today, there are 2 freight railroad companies hauling goods on 1,192 miles (1,918 km) of track in the state. The most common goods hauled by rail include coal, concrete, chemicals, minerals, and petroleum products.

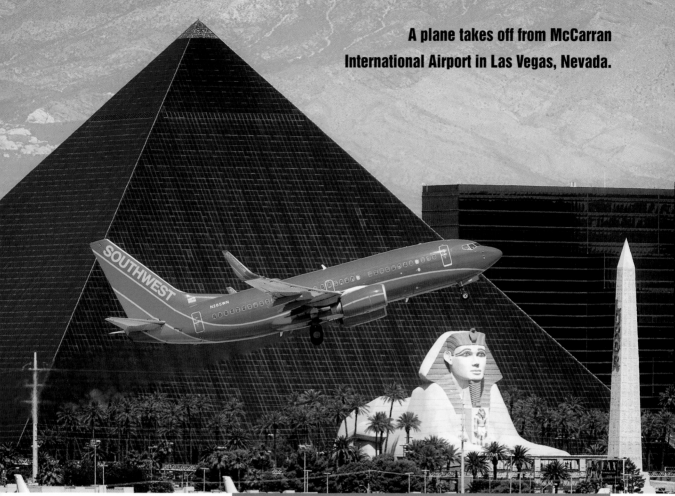

A plane takes off from McCarran International Airport in Las Vegas, Nevada.

Air travel is very important because of Nevada's large size. The state

McCarran International Airport in Las Vegas.

has 6 commercial airports, and about 120 smaller airfields. The busiest airports include McCarran International Airport in Las Vegas, and Reno-Tahoe International Airport in Reno. McCarran International is the first place many tourists see when vacationing in Nevada. It handles about 41 million passengers each year.

TRANSPORTATION

NATURAL
RESOURCES

More than 150 years ago, mineral wealth catapulted Nevada into statehood. Today, precious metals are still important to the state's economy. Nevada is a top producer of gold and silver. Also mined are minerals used in electronic goods, including lithium, iron, and molybdenum. Other minerals found in Nevada include copper, barite, mercury, tungsten, gypsum, limestone, plus sand and gravel.

About 5.9 million acres (2.4 million ha) of Nevada are used as farmland. There are about 435,000 head of cattle in the state. Most graze on Nevada's vast rangelands in the summer. There are also approximately 60,000 sheep.

A geothermal power plant outside of Reno, Nevada. Geothermal power uses underground heat produced by the Earth to generate electricity.

Nevada has about 4,200 farms and ranches. The most valuable crops include hay, alfalfa, wheat, corn, garlic, potatoes, and onions. Most plants are watered by irrigation, either through underground drilling or diverting water from rivers.

Nearly 85 percent of Nevada is owned by the United States federal government, more than any other state. The government uses much of the land as wildlife refuges, for military operations, or to lease to ranchers and miners.

Nevada gets 90 percent of its energy from outside the state. There is some oil and natural gas production, as well as wind, solar, geothermal, and hydroelectric power.

INDUSTRY

Mining and cattle ranching were Nevada's most important industries in the 1800s and early 1900s. They are still important, but the state's economy today depends more on tourism and entertainment. Tourism is Nevada's number-one industry. Visitors spend billions of dollars in cities like Las Vegas and Reno. Approximately 54 million people visit Nevada each year.

Nevada's economy isn't all fun and games. The state's businesses manufacture many kinds of products. They include electronics, chemicals, industrial machinery, paper and printing products, textiles, plastics, and transportation equipment. Food processing is also important. Most manufacturing takes place in southern Nevada, in and around Las Vegas.

Tourists spend billions of dollars each year in Nevada.

Besides manufacturing, other top employers in Nevada include businesses involved in transportation, utilities, business services, education, and health services.

Because the United States federal government owns and controls about 85 percent of Nevada's land, there are many government jobs available. Thousands of military personnel are stationed in the state. Creech Air Force Base and Nellis Air Force Base are two large bases near Las Vegas. Naval Air Station Fallon and Hawthorne Army Depot are in western Nevada.

Planes from Nellis Air Force Base fly over Las Vegas.

SPORTS

There are no professional major league sports teams in Nevada. Minor league teams include the Las Vegas 51s (baseball), the Reno Aces (baseball), and the Reno Bighorns (basketball).

Teams from the University of Nevada, Las Vegas, are called the UNLV Rebels. There are 16 men's and women's sports, but the university is best known as a basketball powerhouse. UNLV's rivals across the state are the Nevada Wolf Pack. They represent the University of Nevada, Reno.

"Hey Reb!" is the UNLV Rebels' mascot.

"Wolfie Jr." is one of the Nevada Wolf Pack's mascots.

A cowboy competes in the saddle bronc riding contest at the National Finals Rodeo. The NFR is held each December in Las Vegas, Nevada.

Rodeo is a very popular sport in Nevada, from high school and college on up to professional. Events include bronc riding, steer wrestling, tie-down and team roping, barrel racing, and bull riding. The National Finals Rodeo, held each December in Las Vegas, is the biggest championship rodeo contest in the country. The other big rodeo event is the PBR World Finals, hosted by Professional Bull Riders (PBR).

Las Vegas has long hosted professional boxing title matches. In recent years, Ultimate Fighting Championship (UFC) events have become extremely popular.

Many people enjoy outdoor sports in Nevada, which range from hang gliding to golf. The Lake Tahoe area is especially popular for boating, mountain biking, and hiking.

ENTERTAINMENT

Las Vegas bills itself as the entertainment center of not just Nevada, but the entire country. Reno is also a favorite destination. There are plenty of things to do in both

The Tournament of Kings *show at the castle-shaped Excalibur Hotel and Casino features knights jousting, sword fighting, and racing on horses.*

cities, day or night. Visitors can try their luck at legal gambling, see live entertainment, attend sporting events, eat at fine restaurants, tour museums, and take advantage of the state's many outdoor activities.

Approximately 28 million Nevada visitors venture out to explore state and nearby national parks each year. Red Rock Canyon National Conservation Area is just a few miles west of Las Vegas. There are trails and a road that winds past interesting sandstone formations. Valley of Fire State Park, north of Las Vegas, features red sandstone formations and petroglyphs carved into the rocks by Paleo-Indians long ago. At Great Basin National Park, in east-central Nevada, visitors can see 5,000-year-old bristlecone pine trees, a marble cavern, and 13,063-foot (3,982-km) Wheeler Peak.

Above: Tourists walk through a rock tunnel in the Hoover Dam power plant.
Below: A tour group sees Hoover Dam's massive power-generating turbines.

Nearly one million people tour Hoover Dam each year. It is located 30 miles (48 km) southeast of Las Vegas on the Nevada-Arizona border. The guided tours give unique inner views of the 726-foot (221-m) -tall dam and how it operates.

ENTERTAINMENT

TIMELINE

10,000 BC—Paleo-Indians hunt and gather in today's Nevada area.

Late 1700s—Paiute, Shoshone, Washoe, and Walapai Native Americans occupy the Nevada area.

1776—Francisco Garcés is the first European to explore the Nevada area.

1820s—Trappers and missionaries arrive in Nevada.

1830—The Old Spanish Trail is established.

1843—John Frémont and a group of explorers begin to map the Nevada area.

1848—The United States obtains Nevada from Mexico as a result of the Mexican-American War.

1851—The first European-American settlement in Nevada is established at Genoa.

Virginia City

1859—Silver is discovered in Virginia City. The find is called the Comstock Lode.

1864—Nevada becomes the 36th state on October 31.

1870s-1880s—Low silver prices combine with harsh winters that kill many cattle. Nevada's population drops.

1900s-1920s—More silver and gold strikes in Nevada, along with railroads built across the state, cause the population to rise again.

1936—Hoover Dam is completed.

1940s—Tourist attractions, including gambling and resort areas, are built in Nevada. The state becomes a big tourist destination.

1950s—The United States military builds huge bases in Nevada. Nuclear bomb testing begins.

1962—The military ends above-ground nuclear bomb testing.

1990—The UNLV Runnin' Rebels win the National Collegiate Athletic Association (NCAA) Basketball Tournament.

1997—Andy Green sets the world supersonic land speed record of 763 mph (1,228 kph) in the Thrust SSC in the Black Rock Desert.

2012—The National Museum of Organized Crime and Law Enforcement (also called the Mob Museum) opens in Las Vegas.

GLOSSARY

Bacterial Meningitis

A serious, often deadly, infection of the linings of the brain and spinal cord.

Basin

An area where rivers do not drain into the ocean.

Casino

A place where people go to play games of chance, such as card games or slot machines. Players bet money and hope to win.

Comstock Lode

An extremely rich find of silver and gold in the Virginia Range of western Nevada. Discovered in 1859, it is named after one of the original owners, Henry Comstock.

Great Depression

Beginning in 1929 and lasting into the mid 1930s, the Great Depression was a time when the United States economy was very bad. Many businesses failed, and millions of people lost their jobs. Few people had money to spend.

Mexican–American War

In the 1840s, fighting broke out between Mexican citizens in the Southwest and settlers from the United States. The angry Mexican government told the United States to get its Navy and Army out of California. The United States refused, which led to war. The Mexican-American War lasted from 1846 until 1848. The United States was victorious.

Old Spanish Trail

A route between Sante Fe, New Mexico, and Los Angeles, California. The trail crossed the southern tip of Nevada.

Paleo-Indians

The first residents of Nevada. Most people believe these were the ancestors of modern Native American tribes.

Petroglyph

A carving or drawing on rocks, usually by prehistoric people, for artistic or religious purposes.

Radiation

A stream of particles that emits from a source such as uranium. This energy can cause sickness or be fatal to the people who are exposed to it.

Reservoir

A lake, either man-made or natural, that is often used as a source of water for a nearby city.

Transcontinental Railroad

The first railroad line that stretched the United States, from the Atlantic Ocean to the Pacific Ocean, across the continent. It traveled east and west across the northern part of Nevada.

World War II

A conflict that was fought from 1939 to 1945, involving countries around the world. The United States entered the war after Japan bombed the American naval base at Pearl Harbor, in Oahu, Hawaii, on December 7, 1941.

INDEX